Whirlpoo

Whirlpools of Silence

Poems and Art

By

Patrick J. Leach

ISBN: **978-1484821398**

CreateSpace, North Charleston, SC

Other books by Patrick J. Leach include:

The Tangle of Meanings, A Book of Poetry and Paintings
(Full color print and Kindle editions available)

The Paintings of Patrick J. Leach — Volume One
(Full color print book)

Meditations on the Mysteries of Life, A Book of Poetry and Art
(Color and black & white versions available)

Bare Trees, A Book of Poetry
(Black and white print book and Kindle available)

In This Vast Sea of Stars -Poetry and Art
(Black & white and color print books and full color Kindle available)

The River of Life Poetry and Art by Patrick J. Leach
(Black and white)

Blue (black and white edition) by Patrick J. Leach
Copyright ©2013 by Patrick J. Leach

Acknowledgements

Thanks to Thomas A. Nagy for editing, layout, and for suggestions. Thanks also to Linda Anglin for her help with editing and selection of poems.

This book is dedicated to

THE CREATOR OF EVERYTHING

Patrick J. Leach, 2012, Central Oregon

My website is patleachartist.com

Additional copies of this book may be purchased from Amazon.com and other retailers. Your support is most welcome and appreciated.

Please email me to inquire about purchasing paintings and books, and to offer venues to show my art at galleries, museums and private showings.

Poetry readings are possible. I welcome your participation in helping me share my art and poetry with the world.

Contents

To Have My Soul Agree

How fine it is

To feel ideas

mesh and come together
then come out on a page

to say what is in my mind
to have my soul agree

and let the world

Have these parts of me
I otherwise would hide

By This Old Wall

Men and women gather here to be alone
within themselves

Some cry, some weep red tears

Some connect with perfect strangers, touch,
go away together

No one knows why

By this old wall

But I too feel the melancholy
The utter hopelessness
I call the wall

Some people drop coins and bills
Some ask for help

But everyone feels
what they need most in life

And are left alone to weep

Knowing I'm Not the Only One

We were playing with her little dog outside
    who took my treats at a distance,
    nervous and fearful of me

"It takes a long time for her to warm up and trust anyone"

I laughed, "I'm like that too"

She whispered "Me too"

And we looked at each other and smiled at this big truth
    shared,
    over such a little thing, feeling a little less out of
    place
    in the world

Sometimes so strange in my own skin trying to understand
    why I am the way I am,

    Often not meeting my own expectations
    about how I should be

Knowing I'm not the only one

Lessons

When I was young
We bought paper and balsam wood kites

When the wind blew just right
We'd tie on long cloth tails

To keep them upright
We'd feed out the line

As far as the eye could see
Our little kites

All the way out to the end
Of the thin string line

Imagine how I felt
When the string broke

Knowing it was too far away
With too many houses and

Roads in the way
To retrieve my favorite kite

My first lesson
In letting go

A Place Where Willows Grow

There is a salty red river
Flowing through my head
It carries songs I've never heard
Words fashioned into poetry
Images I cannot clearly see
Rages wild into rapids and waterfalls
Pools steadily into big fishing holes
Where a man can spend a lifetime
Fishing, swimming, waiting for love
To come visit for awhile

And 'round the bend
A place where willows grow
Big lazy drooping trees touch the water
With frogs and dragon flies,
Fireflies at light

It is here, in a little homemade cabin
With a woodstove
I go when life gets crazy
A three-day trip by riverboat
Here it all makes sense
Walking to my swimming hole
For a talk with the fish I do not catch
The hand of God open, welcoming us all
Down by the river most any time day or night
You are welcome to stay awhile
Any time of year is right

The Nexus

At the innermost core

The crucible where important meetings

Take place within my being

Where life-changing decisions are made

Who bears the weight of responsibility?

Who bays in attendance?

Whose votes weight most heavily

Who decides?

Most important of all questions

What weight God is given for the crucial

Decisions: senior partner, junior partner

Or not at all?

At the innermost core of my being

Old Bill

Old Bill sits on his hill, 97 and still kicking,
he chuckles to the wind
"Who would have thought I would live this long?
A miracle the way I lived when I was young"

A gentle breeze, warm and sunny
A million people living in the valley below
"My family owned all this land at one time when
I was young, far as you can see"
He gestured to his great granddaughter, now almost four

"Now we own this hill, down to 40 acres, with money
and factories and buildings in the city,
enough for you and Marie and everybody,
long as you live you are free of poverty."

Bill smiles, she smiles back. "Can we go back now
Grandpa Bill? I'm hungry."

"Sure sweetie," and they slowly walk back to their house
on the hill. Bill smiles, remembering back to when
he walked this way with his grandfather and was told
he'd be taken care of long as he lived.
He was three back then, almost four.

The Coots- 2010

When I Was A Little Boy

Back in the days when I was young I caught frogs
and salamanders with my hands and put bees in jars
to hear them buzz

Butterflies with a net on a stick, rabbits in a snare
but that was no fun; snakes and toads I'd put in my
pocket, spiders too . . . And scare my mom

I loved watching deer too fast to put a hand on
but thrilled to get close and watch them jump and run
Fish were more elusive,
but I'd hook one now and then

Bird's nests explored, robin's eggs light blue speckled
gems, but we dared not touch them, or their mother
would not take them back again

Grasshoppers easy to catch; spit brown tobacco juice
we called it, funny to watch them jump sideways

Flies were fast but some not fast enough.
I'd let them all go in awhile, except the frogs,
built a house for them but when they died I felt bad
never kept them again

Ah, to be that boy again, infatuated, the enchanted
pond in summer, stalking dragonflies, and those
multitudes of creatures we knew so intimately in those
endless days of summer

Summer

Summer is coming
with boats and paddles
fishing rods and tackle boxes

swim trunks and goggles
flip flops, sunscreen
coolers and lawn chairs

swimming pools and rivers
crickets and frog sounds
honey bees and mosquitoes

hiking boots and camp stoves
oh yes, summer is near
I feel it in the air

another summer
to enjoy playing and
relaxing under trees

reading and swatting flies
air conditioners and portable fans
time outside with you

Being With The Bees

Bees visiting the rhododendrons
And azaleas in her garden

She does not visit them

Bees with shiny wings
And furry faces
Friendly as I pull out weeds

We bump; I feel them
Move and fly away
They do not sting

She loves the flowers
Seen through her windows

The wheelchair keeps her in

I'm paid to do work I'd
Do for free

Tending to her gardens
Delighting in early evening breeze
Being with the bees

Broken Clouds

Among my favorite days on earth under

Big puffy white clouds with

Sunshine slanting through

Dark green trees warm

Thinking of you in my life

A good solid woman not so many broken

Dreams and heartaches as some I've known

Promises to myself and God

Life is better now

Putting the emphasis on good and what

God wants for my life puts zip and zing

Back into my days on this

Blue and green planet

Many thanks, many thanks to You

Hope

There are reasons
For everything
Though not everything
Makes sense

New life
With its own time-tables

But I am old
Obscure to it all
Heavy laden
Carrying my own burdens
Trying to fashion life
To meet expectations
With desires

Accepting what comes
Peacefully, though often with a fight

There is hope

When you visit we will stay up late
Catch up on what we've missed
Recalibrate
Consecrate
Greet first light with a kiss
Then plan out our atonement
For all the bad we've done

Where Am I?

Held to a higher standard

I grope for a way out

Being chased in a dream

Fearful for my life

Falling

down

getting up

Wondering why am I still awake?

Where am I?

this planet with molten heart

so geologically active

the dominant life form vicious

warlike creatures I look in

the mirror stare inside my

head I am one of them

groping for a way out

being chased in a dream

wondering why am I here?

My Little Boat, 2011

What Is More Important?

Writing this poem

Or being late for work, again?

Smiling, being kind and generous

Even when I hurt,

Or objecting and disagreeing,

Insulting, crying out?

Living robust heartfelt love-filled days

Or living in fear and despondency, just in case?

Hearing that woodpecker again out somewhere in

The trees, knowing the coyotes are not far away

Even here in the city helps me

Deciding what is more important is easy

When I pause and think of animals drinking

From cool sunlit streams

My place in life is easy

When I let it be

I Am A Broken Man

I crack, fall down
get up
moan and groan
life goes on
doesn't stop
just gets older
I do the best I can
Relax

It's no big deal
one foot out in front
the other follows
this broken vessel
serves me well
it heals
goes on

I crack, fall down
get up
a broken man
this body serves me well
it just gets older
Wiser now, it carries on
the best it can

The Black Dots

the black dots
are hungry
again
wanting something
someone
to feed them
arguing amongst
themselves
imagine thousands
of little black dots
clamoring
arguing turning
upside down
before they sleep
when the lights
go out
hanging
on the floor
fast asleep

Delving In

To the secrets of life

At the tip of my tongue

So close

If only they would come

So long to wait

Such a short time to go

This, all inside me

Delving

In

God Is

God is a glass

Of clean cool water
On a hot sweaty day

God is a smile from a
Stranger passing by, a
Reunion with a friend
Lost long ago

God is forgiveness with
A smile, a long walk
With your best friend
Revealing all your secrets

God is life on earth given
Freely to live as you will
With that special
Spirit you feel within

Trepidation

It was a long trail through the Wilderness Mountains with big green
    trees in a wild river valley

Big red trunks, rocky in places, following rapids and fish-laden pools
    of fresh clear water

Enough wild life about to make me carefully hang my food in trees at
    night

I went alone, along the great Selway River in Idaho; slept on the
    ground in a little triangular zippered tent, carried all my things
    on my back; freeze dried food, a cell phone that would not work

Two weeks in solitude against all good advice; trying to get away from
    myself, being alone with my self if you know what I mean

Saw rattlesnakes, deer, raccoons, coyotes and I think I heard a wolf
    howling late one night. Elk, moose, bear; animals I heard but
    never saw

Pitched my tent, stashed my things inside, and went off the trail,
    wandering with compass and canteen to places people do not
    usually go

Got back to feeling in the moment, worried only about enough to eat,
    wild animals about, whether it would rain or shine, who would
    rescue me if I got hurt and could not walk out

Absent the distant abstract anxiety I carry around not knowing how to
    release in normal life. It felt good to be alive, more real,
    somehow, out there in the wild

Very strange to return to the parking lot on day fourteen, turn the key
    and drive off to the store for potato chips and carbonation, call
    her on the phone in town, thank God I'm alive

Our Man of God - 2010

Coyote

I saw a coyote here on this dead end street in the
        middle of the day; cautious, intelligent, his
        eyes difficult to read

Moving easily right in front of where I was sitting
        in my car parked, writing a poem. Neither
        kind nor cruel, a hunter plain and simple

He looked like a medium sized dog, light brown in
        color, but not a dog, not tame by any
        means and that was evident in the way he
        moved, listened, cocked his head

This is the first coyote I've ever seen up close, an
        intelligent, wary creature as free as you
        and me, three blocks away from where I
        live;

I stand in awe of natural things

A Sacred Place

there are little veins in my thighs
turning permanently blue
tiny hairs on my head turning gray

and this year June is so green and cool,
calm, real, not drunk or stoned

a sacred place to be alive, to be
completely here immersed in this world
going round and round

this one yellow sun
with knowledge there are billions
of them in the Milky Way alone

makes the tiny hairs on my body
stand up to know there are millions
of galaxies, maybe more

this is a sacred place, here, now,
no need to be towed parsecs, klicks,
or light years

it is here, now,
shared with maple through
open window, rain, intensely green

The Stranger

I sat next to her, a stranger, until she spoke, her
insecurities and doubts, her failure to feel connected, that
persistent and compelling sense of separation, not the
deep sense of connection and identification I long to feel.

No rings on her fingers, but a nice friendly face, like she'd
been to the moon and back, alone, ready to try again to
live and be one with the universe and everyone in it.

You know I could relate to her sharing those doubts and
failures to relate to people and groups, alien, breathing in
our hope and connection at times with this group of
outcasts, grateful to be alive, hearing the honesty so freely
given.

And to think I feel that way too, OK, I'm not so
different, a good human being, just like you.

Excused From The Jury

Morning comes early this time of year
The sun a cheerful companion early and late

A pocket full of cash, passport ready to go
Thinking of Europe, Asia, destinations TBA

***

Gene sequencing an inexact science
Who would you love if given the choice of anyone?

Who would you choose if you could pick anyone
In the world to be? Is there reason to refuse this fantasy?

*****

The stars were out thick last night
crowding in on the moon, calling out

But I refused to go outside
laboring inside instead preparing for today

****

The sky is purple with huge filtered sun
wishing I'd gone out and prayed before today

My soul is bared, naked; my body contoured
and vulnerable; friendless, alabaster, blue

Won't you come with me please; we'll travel
around the world, leave our worries behind,
write books and e-books,
make love everywhere we go

Forever

The sun

The stars

Good health

A gentle June rain

Fresh living air

Through the open upstairs window

Eternity whistling happily

Inviting me along

All aboard

We run to catch it

Before it leaves

We take our seats

By the open window

The warm fresh air

Smells so alive

Pass the beauty

Shimmering, believing

We be here forever

Simply change our seats

When the conductor calls

This is your stop

You have to get off

Change stars, change

Beings, eternally, we never die

Just change trains

Change seats

                    Change bodies

                    Change stars

On This Earth - 2006

Driving With Bright Lights On

on that curvy winding ocean road last night
it was so dark and rainy, foggy wherever the road curved
and dipped down low
we drove talking and laughing
feeling warm and secure with the heater and wipers on

you know those bright lights are so welcome
until a car comes the other way
flash theirs when I forget to dim mine
and then the regular lights look so dim

I lie awake thinking how I'd like to have the option of
bright lights in my life, turn them on when I want to see a
little further, brighter, more illuminated for those times
life seems so dark and scary

Good I can slow down or stop for a while
Let others pass when I go too slow
Pull over and close my eyes when I feel sleepy

Pray I find my way home safely
On these dark winding roads of life with God at my side
Knowing all this hurrying will soon enough be over
Let me enjoy this journey while there's still time

Perpendicular

I left the city late last night
Headed east for points unknown

A perpendicular traversing route just pointed the car where
It looked most appealing and drove

To see how far I could get on a tank
full of gas

Planned to stay wherever I wanted
I like the old motels off 2 lane highways

Perpendicular to my normal way of thinking
Made it 500 miles on that tankful of gas

In a town called Rhubarb
Checked into that motel with the flashing neon sign

At quarter past nine in the morning, filled
Her up and ate at the restaurant out back

Think I'll stay here awhile before moving on
See how far I can get on this next tank of gas

Welcome Back

When I went outside tonight it was warm and clear
The moon big and white, smiling back at me,
"Welcome back, it has been awhile"

How can we be moving so quickly around the sun,
Around our axis so fast, with the moon also moving around
Us; how come it does not feel like we are moving at all?

There are things in life I do not understand - even
When I hear the words saying how and why it does not
Feel like that so I do not believe

Thank you moon for smiling back, welcoming me,
Or was it me, following you in that

A Dark Blue Hammock

Hung sturdily between two trees
By a beautiful river where it pools around
The bend between small rapids
The eternal sound of water moving gently over rocks

Sunshine through the green leafed trees
With big brown trunks, oak and willow, grass and
A soft sandy beach
A gentle breeze, 80 degrees

Children swimming in the river
An August watermark full moon hangs high in
The sky barely visible in this light
The sun so bright and yellow, the sky so blue

I am in the hammock softly whistling writing this,
Place unknown, in my mind
Soon to join the others for a swim
Before dinner at the cabins where we've been all week

A beautiful blonde haired woman in a yellow bikini comes
For me, smiling, eyes a deep shade of green, she is so serene
A dark blue hammock on a warm sunny day with you
That's all I need in this fantasy I call my life

The Poetry Reading

Went to the poetry reading at the center today, reluctant, she said, "you'll enjoy it, please go with me."

I acquiesced, muttering as we left.

It was much more interesting and moving than expected, 15 poets mostly hard working blue collar types, four musicians playing guitars and banjos with their poems, and from all but one I felt the honesty and genuine desire to communicate their truths and stories; what does it feel like to be me? Once again, personal witnesses telling what it is to be a human being, not in self-pity or morbid reflection, but stories of courage within their tapestry of friends and family.

I would feel nervous and threatened reading my poetry and performing, believe poetry is best read in solitude, and hide behind that; but I can see why people would like to see and hear the person read her poems as I did today, so grateful they have courage to present themselves to the world in this way.

The Ocean

Is noisy tonight

With the window open

The waves on rocks and sand,

The constant flux

My favorite sounds to sleep by

I feel so hard driven my whole life

Driven hard from within

Demanding success and recognition

But knowing I'm just me

I want to be more like the ocean

Patient, long-lasting, easy on myself,

Supportive of so much other life

Okay with being me

Not the well-known powerful person

I was expected to be

More like the ocean

Happy to just be

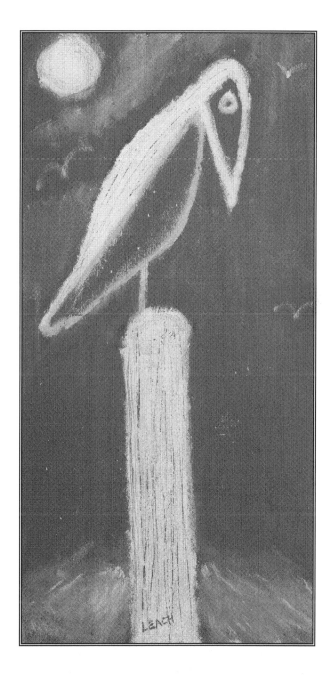

Respite - 2008

The Rock

I felt the power in that northern California coast
Smith River rock, a large ostrich egg shape, gray, worn smooth
by eons rolling on the river bottom, a nice feel to it, powerful, like
it has been used for purposes unknown in the past, collected by
humans perhaps, now in my back yard

There is power in physical things when I open
my mind to see, power and love and perpetuity melding
inanimate and we …

Cripple Creek

water flows high now over rocky rapids

good to drink, clean and pure

the same water that dinosaurs drank

water molecules do not disappear

in you and me now

water does not know or care where it

goes or who it is part of

it freezes solid, flows and pools liquid,

vaporizes into gas it just goes

rain and snow, mist and fog

into the creek it goes into you into me

always through to the next place it

goes on and on for millions

of years

The Citadel

Drooping I entered
The large heavy door

"Private" in small gold raised letters
And lectured those statues

The one armed headless man
The beautiful Cleopatra

Zeus, Hercules, Odysseus
All there, white marble

Listening in rapt attention
While others stared, whispering

"The police are coming,
You'd best be going

Madness has its price
You know"

There are times it is difficult
To decipher real from imagined

The price of life is steep
Essential though, to enjoy its doing

Never afraid what others may think
Or turn to stone, disqualified

They Put You In An Urn

When you were seventeen
After the abortion that ended life
No children now all these years
Fearful of living this way forever
Not knowing who to trust or hate

When men come near you suffocate
Drowning in a river that flows inside
Wondering, wandering all these lonely
Years; is it too late to embrace you now

Help you out of that impenetrable space
They put you in back then
I swear I will try to help
If you'll let me in

Pain First

He will learn pain first, then relief

He will learn what it is to be a man
And stand up on his two feet

Life will teach him lessons and emotions
Will follow, adults will teach him their ways

Always pain first, like being pulled
From the protection of the womb

Into the world with all its problems
To solve and challenges to meet

Pain teaches us lessons, from birth
To the grave

Pleasure teaches, too

May you live your life in pleasure and pain
Peacefully, making the best of what you do

With My Friends

The wind, my friend, played with my hair, pulled it so it stood
on end and frizzed it out; I saw it in the window glass,
I laughed till I cried

With the wind howling in gleeful repose, then the rain,
another close friend, came along, blowing sideways
got me wet, scurrying for cover; now it was a storm
bearing down and I knew it was time for bed

Bamboo heard me hurrying through the wind and rain,
offered shelter and I slipped into cover in the forest of bamboo by the
creek listening to the wind, the rain, the creek water, fluted sounds of
the wind in bamboo and what it told me was this:

"Spend time outdoors with your friends under the sun
and the moon, be one with nature as you are one
with God who sent you, love and joy are your friends
as your life flows from this to the next, all beings are one
in the end; you are here to appreciate nature and all living
things, including you"

The sun rose under broken clouds; it was calm and
warm and I felt joy walking home

As I left bamboo giving thanks I felt God smile in me;
I belong here too, will miss my friends when I go

The City - 2007

The Crucible Of Life

Burns hot and bright

Painful memories of a child abused by alcohol

An insane world full of insane people

Burning guts full of addictions

Smoldering now years later with burned

Out dreams and fantasies

Wondering am I able ever to leave

This world in peace

Meandering, careening, the future will

Consume even you

Selfishness

selfishness

is a weevil

that burrows inside

a man

and sucks his life

until there is nothing

left but thoughts

of what he can get

from everybody

else

and to him it seems

like this is the

only way worth being

always asking

"What's in this for me?"

The Beast Is Still Tonight

Satiated, warm, loved within

Given everything it needs to rest in peace

There is nothing more needed now

All is well

The world rests easy

God is near

Now if only these feelings would continue

A lifetime, I could share them with you

Wouldn't that be nice?

Let it begin

Here

Now

The Fly In Your Soup

1

The flaw in your logic sir, is like a fly in my soup

still flapping its wings; It spoils the idea of eating any more

of it. I can't just take out the fly and eat the soup that way

Your ideas about certain things do that to me

2

I went to a shopping mall tonight for something to eat

Was impressed with the fine clothes and attractive young

people out and about. Sometimes I forget what it was like

to be young and always looking. It is nice to have that

pressure off of me now.

3

I pulled English ivy off the base of huge Douglas fir and cedar

trees today; two hours of old fashioned labor. Could feel

them relax a bit to have this enemy kept at bay.

There are enough things in life to deal with; imagine what it

is like to be stuck in one position at the mercy of tiny insects,

plants and animals that can move and get in your way,

helpless to fight or turn them away no matter how big and

powerful you are

Moments of Peace

Working outside on this warm, tranquil day
Pulling weeds, repairing things

Mind always thinking
Seeking relief in ordinary things of living
Resting my brain for a while

And then the music
Quiet, beautiful notes drifting over me
such a pleasant unexpected surprise

seeing the musician sitting on his deck
a Ph.D. smiling peacefully, eighty four
diagnosed five years ago, advanced

Alzheimer's disease, losing his mind
Does not remember names and most
Particulars, events of his life

And yet he plays such beautiful music
On this glorious summer day
Spent outside

Iris

Thick shallow bulbs

Bursting forth in spring

With sinewy green stalks

In old gardens and flower beds

Followed by gentle warm pigments

Weird shaped flowers unlike any other

The stuff artists fashion on canvas

Abstracted natural beings

I know a woman goes by Iris

Golden yellow hair, sinewy well

Shaped like a man would paint

She plants her namesake in spring, hums

Love songs as she gardens

The kind of woman men dream of loving

Spend their lives dreaming these things

While Iris gardens and sings every spring

Bliss - 2006

Loving a Flesh and Blood Woman

It is a rough situation loving a woman

It brings out the best and the worst in a man

All her imperfections so clarified and real

All his insecurities and extremes emphasized,

Prophesized, trivialized, surreal

So we carry on doing the best we are able

Love is so much more than the lack of our worst

The missing link is love

Links us to God, each other, ourselves

Hotly contested vigilance it is needed

Constantly changing, this is love

Rise and Shine

I woke up with sunshine smiling, dancing, whispering
"Are you awake? It is time for you to rise and shine,
this day divine"

"I give you a beautiful day to live your life, come along
with me dancing between clouds and memories"

What is right for a man to do?
Make peace or war, compassion treats all wounds
Take the slow boat to the islands
Travel light
Swim suit, toothbrush, books to read, books to write
And leave your history behind

Let's start over now
With a credit card, debit card, cell phone, a jacket or
two, pack light
We'll buy what we need along the way

This day is to enjoy, give out what we have, take only
what we need. Sunshine speaking in quiet, earthy well
modulated tones, it is time to live, so rise and shine cast love
about

The Street Fair

Purple ears on the clown saying hello
As we entered the narrow main street
Blocked off to traffic
Sounds of acoustic stringed instruments,
Singing voices, happy music

Craftsmen and women selling their creations
Smiling it is not raining at the coast
Making money when all winter it was sparse
And hard to come by

Oh, the food carts, over here, there spring rolls
And Katmandu, seafood too
We give to you our hearts, our souls, our minds
And worldly goals
Two hours spent wandering here with you
People to watch being with you

The Sound of Singing

Her beautiful voice
So unexpected in this place

I was working outside
From the house next door

Her joy expressing
A hunger, a deep longing

One of our beautiful creations
The human voice singing

With no accompaniment
Only birds singing

A breeze blowing
Her beautiful voice inspiring

And she did not know
I was listening

Your Lips

Your lips are big and red

Your smile wide and sincere

Your hair big and tinted blue

Your eyes are striking greenish blue

Your mind a vast living sea of facts and bright hues

Your body sexy and serene

The way you move

The way you talk

A beautiful lovely walk on the wild side alone with you

Between the human

And the divine

I see you

Your Little Boat

Your little boat is orange
And mine is green

We paddle out where it is serene
Then float where the water goes

Let it take us where it goes
Talking about important things

Then we paddle back
Sit and read relax in peace

Where life is good our weekends
In paradise to enjoy together

You and me and Great Spirit
Laughs and plays with us, comfortably

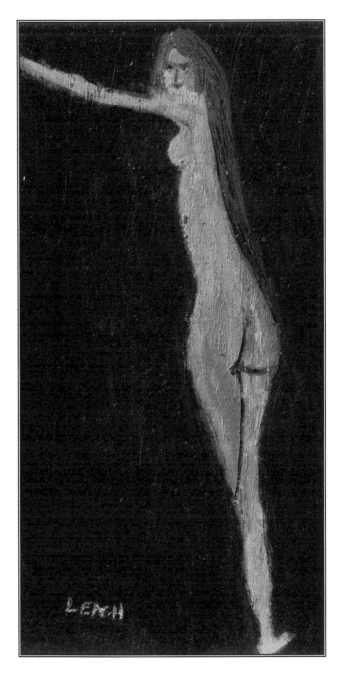

The Black Series / Woman - 2010

A Good Woman

A good woman is hard to find

look below the surface of things

to see into her heart and soul

into her dreams, her fears, her desires

what is she really like inside?

good company even on a bad day?

trustworthy even when you're looking the

the other way?

kind, considerate, passionate, loving

honest even to a fault

like I say, a good woman is hard to find

don't let her go once you find her

or she finds you

Languish

Her entire day "spent in my pajamas, and I'm
not going to leave the house even once"

I smiled, ready to leave her at the door, saying
"I love you" after our weekend together

Languishing away half a day talking about
poetry contests and new books in process, delightful in a
way, but too much to do in two lifetimes or more

Next weekend we spend at the ocean wandering
around, staying on the river where it goes out to sea,
watching the big ocean going ships come and go, making
love, playing cards, relaxing into each other's company

I'm thankful to be me in this huge world of yous, with
one special one to love and love me too, as we languish
happily away together...

Sara's By The Sea

The old wheelbarrow
Retired from carrying things

now at rest as a planter box
with tomatoes, parsley, forget-me-nots
petunias in Sara's front yard

a prominently placed sign
"You are Welcome, Everyone"
near the alfalfa field

where old horses are put out
to pasture, enjoy their last days
and old men come to stay

at Sara's rest home, looking out
at the Pacific Ocean, waves crashing
on rocks with a short sandy beach

hearing the peace all night, windows open
hearing crickets, bees, mosquitoes, birds,
even riding a horse, slowly, when wanted

and buried in the cemetery out back
lies Sara's grave
Sara's granddaughter May

Runs the place now
Visits Sara every day,
Says

"Thank you grandma
For this life by the sea"

A Parking Lot In Paradise

1

We found a parking spot in paradise by the big blue river
      with you, my love, tucked in among the trees and
      picnic tables, walking barefoot along the high trail
      above the old highway where waterfalls thrive and
      people smile automatically
The perfect summer day

Friendly people
With barbeques and family gatherings
Space enough for all

2

and when everybody left we had our dinner at the
      abandoned picnic table in the trees
deer and elk we imagined coming close with their big
      brown eyes
big long trains whistled past, clunk, clunk, clunk, clunk
river boats with their joyous greetings
the sun going down with a parade of colors
more subtle sensual experiences
we felt the peace and longing settle in
meditated and invited Great Spirit in

3

Driving back on the small road out and the big highway home
It seemed like we owned it all to ourselves with the sun sinking
Into the west a day to remember fondly with you
Never quite perfect, but close enough to imagine we'd shared
A nearly perfect day in paradise

Lucy Of The Sea

morning sees you shining with your own
inner light, like the stars

and you turn into the sun rising
sleek and new, pure white teeth when you smile

you are Lucy by day
by night the siren Lorelei

singing and luring men at sea into rocks
under the starry sky

their wrecks breaking up, revealing their
treasures to the light of day

brought up by men from the shallow sea
after you leave to sleep in your cottage in the trees

gold and silver, diamonds and pearls
rubies and emeralds, all manner of precious thing

you know not what fate awaits men lured
by your voice as it sings

only their lustful desires you thrive on those
feelings only you can feel so intensely

your beauty a thing to behold for generations
of men, and the stars shine on rocks and men alike

every night at sea

Trees

Trees are my favorite living beings
So many older and wiser than we

They mind their own business,
give us food shelter, and shade
Provide intangible presence
and peace of mind

I've camped among redwoods,
sequoias, oak, spruce, and noble fir

Hiked through thick forests
of ancient trees

Climbed them as a child
Pulled saplings to the ground
and let them bounce me up high

Never met a tree I didn't love

Wish I could protect them
Nurture and plant more

Our friends the trees of earth

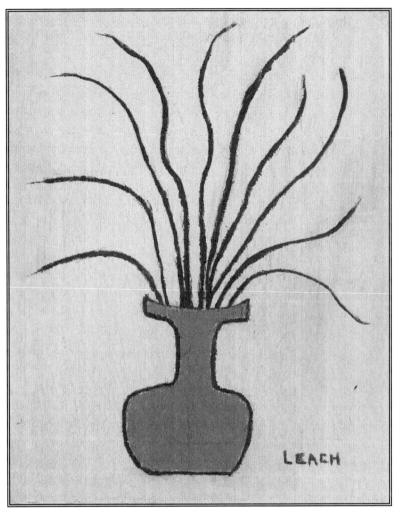

I Feel The Serenity of Birds Singing - 2009

Two Butterflies

Two beautiful butterflies

Flying together

On a perfect summer day

Gently intertwining in flight

Flapping wings to stay aloft

And I imagined one of them was me

What a precious moment

To be alive

A Fishing Story

(as told to me by Bob Wyrick)

My grandfather was quite a fisherman. One evening he went out to his favorite fishing hole, got his rod and reel out and realized he forgot the bait. It was starting to get late and if he couldn't get some bait soon he'd not be able to fish. So he looked around and there in the high grass was a snake with a frog half way into his mouth, still alive.

My grandfather pulled and pulled but couldn't get that frog loose. So he took his pint of whiskey out of his pocket and poured some down into the snake's mouth and sure enough he let go of the frog. Within 10 minutes my grandfather caught a good sized largemouth bass. The frog was of course gone and there was no more bait in sight. So as he was sitting there getting ready to go home he felt a bump on his leg.

He looked down and there was that snake with another frog in his mouth. So my grandfather poured more whiskey down his throat and that snake let loose of the frog. This went on until dark that night. Those snakes in West Virginia are pretty smart when whiskey is to be had for a trade.

The Wind

has always been a friend

brings secret messages for me to hear

comfortable on hot summer days

plays with bells and chimes

makes rivers sing

speaks to me when I need it most

A Gentle Bird Calling

a gentle bird calling

persistent

melodic

amidst all the other

birds calling out

in song and verdant

mysteries

here, where I've seen

the coyote run

by lilac, cedar, oregano

lavender

the woodpecker taps

on trees

like seeks like

in the dance of life

are you dancing?

our choice to sing

or not to sing

to dance or not

to dance

I Can Hear Them Sing

A thin thread holds us together

On each end it joins us to the world

Resilient, nurturing

Weaving our tapestry into so

Much other life with its deafening

Roar, secluded not from

The din within

There are voices calling

Ancestral threads we cannot see

Genes recurring, mysteries

Whispering, repeating

We repeat our tapestry lived before

There are secret things

Live inside our being

When I listen, mindful

I can hear them sing

I Love You - 2007

Aloe Vera

The little aloe vera plant
Sits by my kitchen window

So green and thick at its base
Tranquil there
See smiles at the ready

To heal any wound

    We wink at each other
Each day
She is not needed

    As months
Turn into years
And decades
Follow

And one day
She is

Needed

Hibiscus

In a field of hibiscus

A frog croaks

Wondering

Why me

Here, now

In this place?

Did I choose

This?

Tending the hibiscus,

Hyacinth smiles, nodding

Yes

The mind never

Far away

Persistent

Questions

Multiply like

Eggs

And tadpoles

In July

An Earthwork in Paradise

A beautiful May day

Fresh and warm deep brown moist earth

Digging, and there you were, large, brownish red

I played with you a moment, watched you coil up,

Grow fatter

Moved you to the new garden box I'd just built

And filled with rich compost and earthworm castings,

Topsoil and humus

"An earthworm in paradise" I said as I watched

You burrow in, happy for you in your new home

Lilies

They lie asleep out back

waiting, like us

for Spring

warmth and light

sending them up

from wet brown earth

into deep purple and green

reaching eloquently

toward sky blue light

clouds and rain

they are older than we

will be here in the garden

when we are gone

eternal longing

waiting for the Spring

Forget-me-nots

my love is forgetful

once given and received

so precious then

painful now

rueful treasures

they remain

that gave so

much pleasure

joy perceived

searing pain when they

went away

forget-me-nots

come every spring

blue flowers with bright

green leaves

hardy pleasant beings

forget-me-not the

love you gave

so precious then,

given, and received

The Lily Pad

On the pond in June

bright white flowers sprouting out

families of frogs, some croaking

floating with their eyes just above the surface

little bubbles in the water

tadpoles and dragon flies, mosquitoes

and June bugs

and me in my little boat

my hat down low, paddling

Oh what a fine day to be alive

with the ducks and geese coming nearer

daisies on the shore

the bees in the air

and God right over there

Lovely Jess - 2006

Flowers of Mirth

Thousands of years of evolution

favoring bright colored flowers to attract bees and

humans

Spread joy and happiness, no food value

here, but the smiles multiplying pretty spring days and

lazy summer nights

Give me trees and flowers, bees and joyous

beings, we celebrate our lives to share our Mother Earth

with God and you and me and flowers of mirth

A Lightness of Being

She stuck her tongue out at me

the girl in her mother's shopping cart
I smiled and waved, she giggled and looked
away, her mother's back to me

Shed a heavy feeling I've been carrying around
too long now, and it hit the floor and scurried away
ah, a lightness of being such a pleasure to feel

Like an open window on a warm spring morning
letting in fresh smelling air and the joy of
being alive and well

Those long gone days playing in ditches with swift
flowing water and home made boats
flying kites so far out we could feel the pull on the string

But lost sight of the kite
when nothing interfered with that lightness of being
with the beauty we call God all around

Filling me with a lightness often not felt in my life
some humor on a dark sour day
a little girl smiling then sticking her tongue out at me

As I hurried through my shopping list, paused and
smiled back, remember those days way back when,
when life felt slow and easy so much of the time

The Pictures In My Soul

The pictures in my soul
Nonsequential, faces, places

Landscapes, horses, farms,
Parents, children, God

I love so many,
So many nonsequential things

Myself muted, where turmoil sinks
And airplanes do not take them away

Only when children laugh and play
Does my inner turmoil ever go away

A Windy Reed Pipe

Here, a windy reed pipe spilling over light green and umber liquid intermittent sound

Canary grass in a seed packet waiting for soil and water to begin its new life

There, break open its bonds, a rolling cart collecting trinkets, overflowing always moving, casting about to be friends

Another man, a half bent moon, grumbling how he'd like to change his thinking sufficient to get a room, running water, electric and pay per view

A rather desperate fellow, large hair puffing out about humble beginnings now hugely successful at all he touches, most believe him, struck by cancer and dead before reaching 50

Crabgrass in the family lawn, getting attention for problems, often drama follows his paths all the way home, society pays his bills through family obligation

There another Chaucer if only you'd believe his storefront kiosk, I know the way if you'll follow right this way

Another man, this one old and gray, stroked at 50, plays guitar, writes jokes at 70, gardens for pleasure, sleeps in till noon

Mental illness strikes another, hunger, confusion, without friends or family, holds her social workers at bay "please

leave me alone now, there is nothing wrong with me, just
get away and leave me alone"

So many of us with our odd threadworn personalities,
pianos, tubas, clarinets, gray cats and dogs, violins, cellos,
trumpets, harpsichords, sitars, guitars, drums and castanets

A delicious looking harp player sits, playing sad despondent
notes languishing a lifetime of secret fantasies forever
hidden, no one to love her

I ring my Asian gong morning and night, holding Buddha,
pray my prayers of thanks, write a poem before work,
wonder, when will they turn out the lights?

Dear God

I thank You for giving me this life
I come to You now asking

    Please help me be a kinder, more gentle
    Loving man toward everyone
    Someone people want to trust and be
    Around, less selfish, more giving
    With You truly a bigger part
    Of who I am

    Way deep inside where we live
    And thrive together, making this life
    The best it can be for everyone
    Who comes in contact with me

The Soul In Your Eyes – 2006

Tea Leaves

Tea leaves scattered on the kitchen table
Green and black, undecipherable to me

The dark haired older woman with makeup
Smeared on a tearful face, confused, crying out
For help, blinded

"What did you see in the tea, tell me
please?" I ask

She turns but her eyes are closed, crying
"Help me, I must get out of this place, please
help me out of here now"

I grasp her hand, stained green and black,
"Do not return to this place or you will face the end
with me"

She falls, I cannot hold her up, call 911, give
CPR, when the ambulances arrive I run away, never
To return again to this tragic scene with the sign out
Front "Fortune Teller"

The Metronome

Ticks,

Blends

With the ever present

Background

Noise

Being

Alive

Engenders

Takes its toll

And just when

I feel

I am at peace

With each

And every thing

The terror

The utter unmanageability

Strikes

Deep into me

Just another

Day alive

This Too Shall Pass

The young man scratching his prison cell wall marking
    time, wishing it would pass more quickly, getting
    older and wasting his youth locked away

Sailors gambling in the evening to pass their time tending
    tankers and cargo ships, paid by the crossing,
    hating their jobs but needing the money

Patients suffering chemotherapy debating to themselves,
    quietly muttering, "How can I survive this misery
    that may not even work?"

This too shall pass, the joy and celebrations, the pain and
    remorse, everything changes and eventually goes
    away

Time heals all things, phrases conveying wisdom that hold
    their meaning over all generations

A lifetime lived looking back, knowing this too shall pass
    with all its triumphs and regrets;

Loving and giving of oneself always holds enduring value,
    and this too shall pass

Julius

Sweeping up the mess with the old fashioned broom
and dust pan

What does a man need to clean up the mess
inside his mind?

Emotional debris, a lifetime is a long time
to build up, and clean

    ***

He carries it all so secretly, no one
seeing would ever know his pain

    ****

The starlings and crows gather up close
looking, seeing, seeking a bite to eat

And they found a man dying in the heat
on the ground under the juniper tree

Moaning, whispering his cries for help
the birds sat up in the trees, silently
waiting for him to die

    *****

Junipers and sagebrush languishing out here,
everywhere the water does not reach

The rattlesnake has eyes that see everything
he waits patiently for someone's mistake
a hunter extraordinaire

Never fear, a warm meal is not far away

He is cold blooded
rattles to let you know he is near
tells you he will strike if you get too near

    ******

And in the end Julius did not die

He went back to the house, brought water
and food for the birds, got back into his
routine, doing what comes naturally to him,

A kind loving man who had the fright
of his life, time to take his pills and
be glad he's alive . . .

I Can't Remember

There were so many days and nights alone
With bone-chilling pain when I thought
Of wrongs I'd done with her

History cannot be changed or altered
Always we wear the same; a different fit

My mind is numb

I knew a man who would proclaim,
*"I'm bad at relationships; I live my life alone;
I'll not mess up anyone's life but my own."*

How comforting it must be to be so sure of what you know,
you will not change your ways. In his case, how all alone . . .
or did he change his mind?

Some of us say things with great certainty
Then turn around and change.

I've been there, so I should know.
If only I could remember.

Weeping

the tears flow

    down

    in

    my

    soul

    deep
    into
    the
    bottom of who I am

    circling around

    before they

    rise up

    again

Please Help Me

I lost my way more than once

I almost lost my soul

Who can help me

Prosper, live free of waste

And poverty of soul

Like the time in London an older well dressed man

Handed me 10 British pounds in heavy sterling

Unbidden, no reason given

He smiled and walked away

And I was younger then

Now the stakes are higher

The need seems greater

So close to knowing what is true

With time running out

Please help me find my way

Fulfill my reason for being here

Before I'm called back home

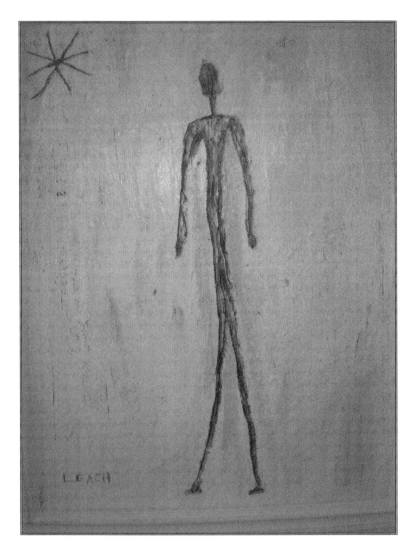

Every Man, 2010

A Ridiculous Man

Praying for good weather to work outside
Jobs that pay

A loving woman, peace with her
Asking God for so much

Pretending deep concern for other beings
Wanting sincerely to be this way

Getting up in the morning, thinking, always thinking
Late at night his favorite time of day

Sleeping, silent, mind peaceful
Soul at rest, dreaming

There are beautiful sunny calm waking moments
Wrapped in love, grateful to live, alive

Lazy heartfelt moments that quench his thirsty soul
Give hope and life something back

Those thank you moments that go down
In life's journal of prayers, sacred

Moments even a ridiculous man treasures
When we walk with Great Spirit hand in hand, equally

A Veteran In Need

The gutter is a lonely place
3 bottles in hand, paid for in cash for more cheap
fortified Thunderbird wine, last night it was Ripple

after a half day out in the rain at the freeway exit
smoking home rolled cigarettes
with a sign, "Veteran in Need"

and one guy gave him a twenty and some weed
so it's off to his hiding place in the bushes
between two roads out back

near EM's for more alcohol, police do not go there
too dangerous unless there's a need
he looks forward to a night alone with the wine

and the weed, smoking, not knowing this is the
night he will die on his way to his lonely hideout
with a knife in his throat

over 2 bottles of rot-gut and a small bag of weed
buried 2 feet deep in a shallow unmarked grave
a veteran in need

Yoga

An alignment

When I was out of whack

Bending, stretching,

Breathing, meditations

Asking God to come

Back in

In alignment

Feeling human

Once

Again

Star Gazer

Thomas gazes up at the stars
A fresh shot of sorrow and pain running
Through his veins
Tears running down his face,
Dripping on his feet
"Why is this happening to me,
again?"
The wind blows off the sea, gently,
Waves playing persistent melodies, lonely
Tonight.
It is warm and clear, after weeks
Of rain and wind, something calling out:
"Fear not what you cannot change,
everything will change, know joy once
again, let me help you Thomas, friend."
Thomas lay down on the sand, went
To sleep and had peaceful dreams, woke
With the sun coming up and happiness in
His heart to begin another day

God Bless You

The stars are whispering tonight
"The work is done, come out and play with us"

It is peaceful and calm inside
Rest and sleep welcoming me to stay in

How we go beyond mortal things?
Give emancipation from self a fling

I travel to the stars tonight
Close my eyes and open my mind

God bless you
Each and every one

Everywhere
Everything

The Hinges Creak

The hinges creak

I know you are coming in

Unannounced, uninvited

A mile is a long way to walk

Without shoes or socks

Barely able to resist falling asleep

On your feet

How many trees does it take

To agree this is a forest

Please take great care of yourself

People will try to bring you down

In a few more days we will be free

Of all this obscurity

Brought on by over work

And under pay

So Many Stars - 2005

The Trouble With Too Much To Do

It is said

People are too stressed out

Too much to do

Too little time

Now showers are the thing

Quick and easy

I enjoy my evening soak

Luxuriate, read a book

Close my eyes

Free my mind

Before I go to bed

It relaxes me

Prepares me for another day

As I drive to work

So much to do

Until the evening soak

Something to look forward to

Under The Ice

The river freezes close to the shore every winter,
Starts out with an almost imperceptible film
On the surface, fun to touch and hear it crackle

Then it snows, builds up snow on ice, ice grows thicker,
Not uniform, all wavy and inconsistent, fun to explore
When it gets thick enough we run and play on the ice

Watch out for those strange places like bubbles
Where a body can fall through and go under the ice
We've heard stories of what can happen if a man falls under

The ice and can't find his way out. One day, a clear sunny
Day just past two when the sun goes down around five. I
Was out at the edge of the ice, where it meets the blue liquid
Water

It is fun to hear the cracking of the ice where it joins the river
And a big chunk let loose and there I was floating on the
Water on a big chunk of ice heading out into the open water,
Concerned now

What is happening to me? I cannot jump in and swim to
Shore with the ice blocking my way. If I stay on the ice flow
Where will it go?

No phone, no rescue in sight.

And then I awake. Knowing full well when I was young
I saw this had happened to a deer heading out toward
Niagara Falls, rescued by Navy Island and a whole herd of
Deer waiting to play

Sound Asleep In My Warm Dry Bed

I dream of being with you feeding
Baby ducks and their mothers,

Playing Frisbee, laughing when it
Goes in the creek or over the fence

Sitting on the park bench in the shade
Trying to meditate with the ducks

Quacking close by, talking quietly,
Smiling, making plans for future gatherings

All this in a dream
It is that summer of eleven all over again

Writing poetry, painting abstract people
Working my job outside

Enjoying life as it was meant to be
Even in my dreams, with you and You and me

Silly

Silly

                Infestations
    Of words
       Held high
Like hornets
     Going   into a nest
        In the   family
           Tree

Moths   bouncing off   the
                           Light
                           Out
                           Back

People driving
    Their cars
        With cell phones
    Eating sandwiches
        Eyes drop between
     Stops
   Sunglasses hide
What's going on inside

You and me
    Going into our homes

    Hiding from the summer

    The police
       And all that we

Would rather not see

We of Earth and God - 2006

Whirlpools Of Silence

downstream where the
river bends sharply
and the rapids run out
there are whippoorwills
and geese, ducks, beaver
and deer come to drink
there are little whirlpools
and eddies where the river
plays and birds congregate
to mate
whirlpools of silence
eddy here at first light
     I come here then
to listen to the silence
condense into morning
as the stars fade away
no longer bright, time slows
to a trickle, holding all the
world in one long still moment
of peace until overtaken by
 the day
     we are all equal now
our mother earth's children
I wish we could stay this way

Index of Paintings